A real friend will be more loyal
than a brother.

PROVERBS 18:24 NCV

For you, my friend,

_____

with love,

_____

date

_____

We have been friends together
in sunshine and in shade.

CAROLINE NORTON

The BEST FRIEND in the WORLD

HOWARD BOOKS

A DIVISION OF SIMON & SCHUSTER

New York   London   Toronto   Sydney

Our purpose at Howard Books is to:

- *Increase faith* in the hearts of growing Christians
- *Inspire holiness* in the lives of believers
- *Instill hope* in the hearts of struggling people everywhere

Because He's coming again!

Published by Howard Books, a division of Simon & Schuster, Inc.
1230 Avenue of the Americas, New York, NY 10020
www.howardpublishing.com

HOWARD
BOOKS

The Best Friend in the World © 2007 by Dave Bordon & Associates, LLC

Library of Congress Cataloging-in-Publication Data

The best friend in the world / [edited by Chrys Howard].
     p. cm.
  Includes bibliographical references.
  ISBN-13: 978-1-4165-4175-2
  ISBN-10:   1-4165-4175-6
  ISBN-13: 978-1-58229-695-1 (gift ed.)
  ISBN-10:   1-58229-695-2 (gift ed.)
  1. Friendship—Religious aspects—Christianity. I. Howard, Chrys, 1953–
  BV4647.F7B47 2007
  242—dc22
                            2007015582
10 9 8 7 6 5 4 3 2 1

Manufactured in the United States of America

For information regarding special discounts for bulk purchases, please contact: Simon & Schuster Special Sales at 1-800-456-6798 or business@simonandschuster.com.

Project developed by Bordon Books, Tulsa, Oklahoma
Project writing and compilation by Shawna McMurry and Christy Phillippe in association with Bordon Books
Edited by Chrys Howard
Cover design by Lori Jackson, LJ Design

Every effort has been made to obtain and provide proper and accurate source attributions for selections in this volume. If any attribution is incorrect, the publisher welcomes written documentation supporting correction for subsequent printings.

CONTENTS

Oh, the comfort, the inexpressible comfort of

feeling safe with a person, having neither to weigh thoughts

nor measure words, but pouring them all out, just as they are,

chaff and grain together, certain that a faithful hand will take

and sift them, keep what is worth keeping, and with

a breath of kindness, blow the rest away.

DINAH MARIA MULOCK CRAIK

INTRODUCTION

Friendship is among the most precious gifts we are given to enjoy in life. Through friendship, we gain insight into ourselves and others. A friend is a safe haven for our secrets, a source of comfort in our trials, and a wellspring of immeasurable joy. Through our friends, we're able to experience firsthand the wonder of giving and receiving unconditional love.

The Best Friend in the World celebrates the joy of friendships everywhere, but most especially, it honors you, the unique and special friend in my own heart. I hope this book inspires, encourages, and shows my appreciation to you, my treasured friend. I'm so honored and thankful that God has placed you in my life.

My dear friend, you're the best!

You're the
BEST
FRIEND
in the World Because…

You're Always

There for Me.

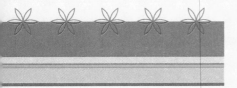

There are times when I
want to share my life's
triumphs and tragedies
with someone, but none
will do except the hearing
ear of a good friend.

R. M. KITE

A friend loves at all times.

PROVERBS 17:17

Friendship is, perhaps, one of the greatest marvels of God's creation. We are not born into friendships as we are into families. We have a choice of whom we will befriend, or even whether or not we will allow friends into our lives. Yet God has wired us with an innate need for friendship, and for good reason. How much we would miss in life without this precious gift.

We are best able to put into practice the principles of loving others through our friendships, and in these relationships, we discover the reality and meaning of unconditional love. We are able to experience in concrete form the love God has for us and the kind of relationship He desires to share with each of us.

Treasure your friendships. Feed them with your time, energy, love, and prayers. In the end, the relationships you've formed with others—your friends and family—will be your greatest assets and are the only earthly commodities you can take with you into eternity.

A LETTER TO MY FRIEND

Dear Friend,

You're always there for me when I need you the most. Life gets busy, and we don't always get to talk to each other as often as we'd like. But no matter how much time passes between our conversations, we always seem to be able to pick up just where we left off. I know I can always count on you to be available with a listening ear and a caring heart. And I know I'm often in your prayers, as you are in mine.

When I have a problem and can't figure out what to do, you're only a phone call away, and you never fail to have some wise words for me. When you have some exciting news, you're quick to share it with me and let me take part in your joy. When either of us needs someone to be there to help the other with a difficult situation, no distance is too great for either of us to travel.

Thank you for being such a faithful, constant friend to me.

Love,

Your Friend

My friends have made

the story of my life.

In a thousand ways they

have turned my

limitations into beautiful

privileges, and enabled me

to walk serene and happy in

the shadow cast by my

deprivation.

HELEN KELLER

It's the friends you can
call up at 4:00 a.m. that matter.

MARLENE DIETRICH

ALWAYS THERE FOR ME

By Julie Morrison

You weren't afraid to be there for me when I stumbled through an unwanted divorce. You let me cry and hurt and try to make sense of it all. You didn't say, "It will be okay." You said, "The Lord will never leave you or forsake you."

You didn't let me slip too far when I was losing control of my daughter. I felt she'd been through a lot. I wanted her happiness and caved in to her too often.

You didn't say, "That's okay. She'll be fine." You said, "Children need discipline, and don't worry if she hates you now. She'll love you later." You were brave enough to show me where I needed correction. I welcomed and trusted your advice.

When hard times hit me, you didn't say, "You're like a cat— you'll land on your feet!" When I had no gas in my car to visit my dying father in the hospital 100 miles away, you dropped everything to come over and give me money for traveling. When I didn't have food, you took me to the store every Tuesday for groceries. When my mother abandoned me, you hugged me and loved me like your own child. You invited us to your home for holidays and treated us like family. When my faith felt thin, you gave me verses, encouraging words, and prayed with me. When sad days came, you shared in my pain. When I felt lonely, you took me out for coffee every week to talk.

Two years of Tuesdays later, after groceries, over coffee, I asked you, "What kind of man do you see me with?" You didn't say, "Adventurous, drop-dead gorgeous, artistic, or rich." You said, "One who just adores you the way you are, who loves your daughter and loves God." As the words sank in, God revealed my husband-to-be in the coffee shop that day: a kind and gentle man who talked with me before service every week at church.

When good things happened, you shared in my joy. When I asked you to be in our wedding the next year, you said, "I wouldn't miss it for the world!" And my dad, who had miraculously survived and recovered, gave me away at my wedding as you watched with tear-filled eyes.

Now my daughter is happy and says she wants to be like me. My new husband and I laugh a lot, often shop together at the grocery store, and go out for coffee and talk. We attend church as a family.

I am blessed because of you. Because of your love and encouragement, I made it to the other side of hardship and trials. Because you invested in me, I want to invest in others with the same dignity, grace, and compassion you gave me.

Because you love me like family, you are the best friend in the world.[1]

There is nothing on this
earth more to be prized
than true friendship.

WHY I'M THANKFUL
YOU'RE MY BEST FRIEND…

…You've solved more
fashion emergencies than
I'd care to admit.

We are not primarily put on the earth to see through one another, but to see one another through.

PETER DEVRIES

✼ ✼ ✼ ✼ ✼

Heavenly Father,

You are my best friend, and You've given me a wonderful example of what a true friend is. What I treasure most about our friendship is that You're always there for me anytime I need to talk or share my excitement or just need a shoulder to cry on. You're never too busy to build on our relationship.

Help me follow Your example in my friendships with others. Make me sensitive to my friends' needs, and help me to know when my presence can be a source of comfort, strength, or encouragement for them.

I've known the peace that comes from having that friend I can call on anytime, night or day, and also the pure joy of being able to be that person for another. I don't want to miss even one of those opportunities because I've become too busy with the tasks of everyday life.

Thank You for Your friendship and for the many friends You've placed in my life.

Amen.

I THANK GOD for you,

my LOYAL friend!

You're the
BEST
FRIEND
in the World Because...

You Make Me

Laugh.

Laughter is the best medicine
—a friend the best to dispense it.

D. Valentine

❋ ❋ ❋ ❋ ❋ ❋ ❋ ❋ ❋ ❋ ❋ ❋ ❋ ❋ ❋ ❋ ❋ ❋ ❋ ❋

[A virtuous woman] is clothed with strength and
dignity; she can laugh at the days to come.

PROVERBS 31:25

When you think about friendship, some words that may come
to mind are *loyalty, caring, thoughtfulness, honesty.* These are
all essential ingredients to a good friendship. But have you
ever really stopped to consider the important role laughter
plays in our friendships?

Proverbs 17:22 calls a cheerful heart "good medicine." Your
ability to laugh with your friends can be not only a source of
enjoyment for them but also a healing balm for wounded hearts.

In the list of qualities of a virtuous woman found in Proverbs
31, you'll find laughter right up there with strength and dignity. The woman described in this passage is busy, to be sure.
Yet one of her most admirable qualities is her ability to laugh
and find joy in the midst of her busy days.

So take some time out today to share a laugh with a friend. It
may be just the thing you both need to make it through the day.

❋ ❋ ❋ ❋ ❋ ❋ ❋ ❋ ❋ ❋ ❋ ❋ ❋ ❋ ❋ ❋ ❋ ❋ ❋ ❋

A TRIBUTE TO MY FRIENDS

There's nothing else quite like sharing laughter with good friends. Some of my strongest bonds of friendship were formed in college, during late-night "study" sessions that turned into giggle sessions instead. It was during these times that we learned how to relax and take ourselves less seriously, to laugh at ourselves and at our circumstances. Sharing laughter made the pressures we were facing seem much smaller, and somehow all the important things still got done, but with a smile rather than tears.

Years later, we still take time out at least once a year to get together, and when we do, there's always lots of laughter. We talk about plenty of serious things—hardships we've encountered, hopes diverted, and hurts we've experienced along the way. But as long as we have each other, life is never so serious that we can't enjoy a good giggle session.

Lord, I thank You for my friends who are so willing to share the gift of laughter and for the new life and strength I find in their presence.

S. D. RICKARD

Joy is the echo

of God's life within us.

JOSEPH MARMION

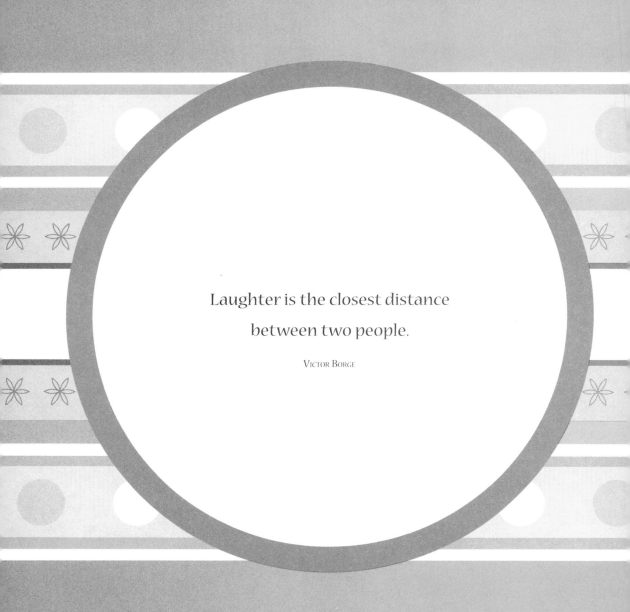

Laughter is the closest distance

between two people.

Victor Borge

HUNTERS AT HEART

By Carol McAdoo Rehme

"Do you remember where we parked the car this time?" I chewed my lower lip.

My friend, Vic, scanned the street to the north, made an abrupt about-face, and looked south. "Well, how far do you think we walked? And which direction did we come from?"

Who knew?

Broadway boasted block after block of quaint secondhand stores, dim pawn shops, and burgeoning antique malls. Ever sisters in adventure, we had diligently sampled them all. For hours on end. With lunch squeezed somewhere in between.

"Not again," I groaned. Twice during the day, we'd returned to move the car up (or was it down?) the street. Once, just far enough to avoid a ticket for parking too long in the same space. And again, to deposit an armful of purchases and a hefty nightstand (burled oak with original hardware). Both times I'd forgotten where I'd left my white Subaru Outback, a vehicle, it seemed, with as many look-alikes as there was reproduction enamelware.

"Uh, you're a bit directionally challenged," my friend had teased as we scoured each side of the street until we found the car.

Neither of us was familiar with Denver. But our timidity of the daunting city was overshadowed by our insatiable lust for all things old, the thrill of the hunt, and the dogged determination to worm our way through every last store on Broadway (do or die).

From the pain of my swelling feet, I figured the *do*ing part was pretty much done. Now I was ready to die.

"Vic, we've *got* to find the car. It's getting dark. And it's nearly time for dinner."

"I'm sure you left it there." She pointed toward the dusky shadow of the mountains. "South."

"Uh, that's west." I laughed and limped down the street.

"We're a sorry pair," Vic muttered.

After two blocks and thirty minutes (we discovered one store we hadn't yet been in), it was obvious to both of us that we should have walked north. We turned back. Four long blocks later, I held my breath while I hobbled to the car.

"Let's eat along the way," I suggested. "It's a long drive home."

Afraid to stray far from a main roadway, we stopped at the first restaurant we saw (parking near the door, where we could find the car!). We lingered over our tasty meal (Mexican, with sopapillas for dessert).

"Well, let's hit the restroom and head out," I suggested with a yawn.

And it was there, inside the little room marked *Senoritas,* that Vic and I finally realized our friendship was based on much more than our shared love for antiques. She dried her hands, opened the door—and walked right into a broom closet!

We are both, we decided, directionally challenged.

We think it may be genetic—a faulty gene that friends inherit from each other![2]

❋ ❋ ❋ ❋ ❋

Among those whom
I like or admire,
I can find no
common denominator,
but among those
whom I love, I can:
all of them make me laugh.

W. H. AUDEN

WHY I'M THANKFUL
YOU'RE MY BEST FRIEND…

…You always send me the
most hilarious birthday card.

Laughter is the sun that drives winter from the human face.

VICTOR HUGO

✵ ✵ ✵ ✵ ✵

Heavenly Father,

Thank You for the gift of laughter. What a great feeling it is to share a laugh with a friend over something we both find comical! There's something about laughter that helps us feel connected and understood. It has an almost supernatural quality that spreads joy to anyone who hears it. It helps us forget about our worries and the heaviness of our responsibilities.

Thank You for placing friends in my life who are good about helping me lighten up when I become too serious and who graciously laugh at my silliness. When I start to let the stresses of life get to me, all I need is an evening with a few of my friends to feel refreshed and ready to face a new day. Whether we watch a movie, work on a craft or scrapbook project, or just hang out and talk, we always find plenty to laugh about; and soon my worries seem silly in comparison to all the goodness You pour into my life.

When I forget, keep me mindful of the healing qualities of laughter and the wonderful friends who bring its music into my life.

Amen.

I THANK GOD for you,

my JOYFUL friend!

You're the

BEST

FRIEND

in the World Because...

You're
Kindhearted and
Forgiving.

Forgiveness is the act of offering what
we also need for ourselves.

Emma B. Cloud

> *Bear with each other and forgive whatever grievances you may have against one another. Forgive as the Lord forgave you.*
>
> COLOSSIANS 3:13

No matter how considerate friends may be toward each other, forgiveness is an essential part of any relationship. We sometimes unknowingly offend others simply because of differences in our upbringing or personalities. But these occasions can become opportunities for our friendships to grow deeper, strengthened by the bonds of graciousness and forgiveness.

Showing grace toward a friend who has offended you is a great way to demonstrate God's love and His forgiveness. If you have a friend who has done something that didn't set well with you, don't let your feelings fester. If you need to, confront that person, and then offer your forgiveness and put the matter to rest. If you feel you've offended a friend, don't avoid the situation. Instead, do all you can to make the matter right.

Friendships are too valuable to throw away because of petty disagreements. And you may be surprised at how far a little forgiveness can go.

A LETTER TO MY FRIEND

Dear Friend,

I was late to my own birth and have been late to just about everything else since. But you never hold this fault of mine against me. Instead, we just have an understanding that any time we get together, our plans start thirty minutes after the agreed-upon meeting time. You lovingly laugh at my forgetfulness and take it in stride when my daughter makes the occasional sassy comment to yours, never judging my parenting abilities but trusting me to correct the situation.

Thank you for being forgiving and patient with me. By doing so, you reflect God's unconditional love and complete acceptance of me, faults and all. My prayer for you is that you'll receive from others the same grace you so willingly give.

Love,

Your Friend

Forgiveness is a funny
thing. It warms the heart
and cools the sting.

WILLIAM ARTHUR WARD

Forgiveness is the sunshine that

erases the dark shadows from the soul.

VALENCIA SMITH

MAY BASKET

BY SUE DUNIGAN

"Hey, do you know what? Today is May Day!" my sister announced. "Do you remember the May Day baskets we used to make with colored paper and paste?"

Childhood memories and warm feelings engulfed me as I recalled that my sisters and I would run around our neighborhood delivering the not-so-perfect baskets brimming with spring flowers. We would place the handmade treasures on a doorstep, knock on the door, then scurry away as fast as our legs would carry us. It was delightful to peer around a bush and watch our friends open their doors and pick up the colorful gift, wondering who had left it out for them.

I distinctly remember the May Day of the year that I was in fifth grade. That year I was faced with a challenge involving one of my dearest friends. She lived right across the road from our family, and we had walked together to school nearly every day since first grade.

Pam was a year older than I, and her interests were starting to change from the interests that we had shared together. A new family had recently moved into our small town, and Pam was spending more and more time at their house. I felt hurt and left out.

When my mother asked me if I was going to take a May Day basket to Pam's house, I responded angrily, "Absolutely not!" My mom stopped what she was doing, knelt down, and held me in her arms. She told me not to worry, that I would have many other friends throughout my lifetime.

"But Pam was my very best friend ever," I cried.

Mom smoothed back my hair, wiped away my tears, and told me that circumstances change and people change. She explained that one of the greatest things friends can do is to give each other a chance to grow, to change, and to develop into all God wants each of them to be. And sometimes, she said, that would mean that friends would choose to spend time with other people.

It was a hard decision, but I decided to give Pam a basket. I made an extra special basket of flowers with lots of yellow because that was Pam's favorite color. I asked my two sisters to help me deliver my basket of forgiveness. As we watched from our hiding place, Pam scooped up the flowers, pressed her face into them, and said loudly enough for us to hear, "Thank you, Susie. I hoped you wouldn't forget me!"

That day, I made a decision that changed my life: I decided to hold my friends tightly in my heart, but loosely in my expectations of them, allowing them space to grow and to change.[3]

＊　＊　＊　＊　＊

Lord,

Your patience with me and Your continual forgiveness are overwhelming. Not only do You forgive me when I mess up, but You've also given me wonderful friends who are willing to do the same. When I do something wrong or offend them in some way, they don't judge me for it or hold a grudge. They're good about being honest with me and telling me what I need to hear, but they do it in a spirit of love and not of revenge or anger.

Help me to always be as quick to forgive. When I have a conflict with a friend, help me to know the best way to handle it, being both honest and sensitive to my friend's feelings. If I ever do something to offend a friend without knowing it, please make me aware of what I've done so I can work toward a solution.

As I grow in my friendship with You, walking in the assurance of Your grace, I learn to be a better friend to those around me. Thank You for friends who are walking with You and learning from You as well.

Amen.

I THANK GOD for you,

my kindhearted and FORGIVING friend!

You're the
BEST
FRIEND
in the World Because...

You're So

Thoughtful.

Many people will walk
in and out of your life.
But only true friends
will leave footprints in
your heart.

ELEANOR ROOSEVELT

* * * * * * * * * * * * * * * * * * * *

God is able to make all grace abound to you,
so that in all things at all times, having all that you
need, you will abound in every good work.

2 Corinthians 9:8

Just as you love to do thoughtful things for your friends and family, God loves to do thoughtful things for His children. And He does—every day. He's provided you with everything you've needed in order to become the person you are today. He's given you unique talents that have equipped you to be a wonderful friend and to develop meaningful relationships that will last a lifetime. He's supplied you with the time and resources you've needed to do what He's called you to do. And He continues to bless you with new energy, ideas, resources, and inspiration.

As you talk with your heavenly Father today, take a moment to reflect on His thoughtfulness toward you. Thank Him for supplying all of your needs and for the many unique and creative ways in which He's blessed your life.

* * * * * * * * * * * * * * * * * * * *

A TRIBUTE TO MY FRIEND

I have a friend who gives the most thoughtful gifts. One year for my birthday, she volunteered an entire weekend to redecorate my bathroom that had been driving me crazy for years. She and her husband bought paint and supplies, peeled off the ugly wallpaper, and gave my bathroom a much needed facelift. This thoughtful act renewed my tired, busy-mom heart and restored my hope of getting through my lengthy list of home-improvement projects that had long sat dormant.

Another year when we were short on funds, she and her husband treated our family to an all-expense-paid weekend of camping, an activity we greatly enjoy but couldn't afford at the time.

Father, bless my friend for her thoughtfulness and generosity. Inspire me with creative ideas to return her kindnesses.

SHAWNA MCMURRY

A friend's words

are like a cool spring—

they refresh your spirit.

EDWARD J. MOFFAT

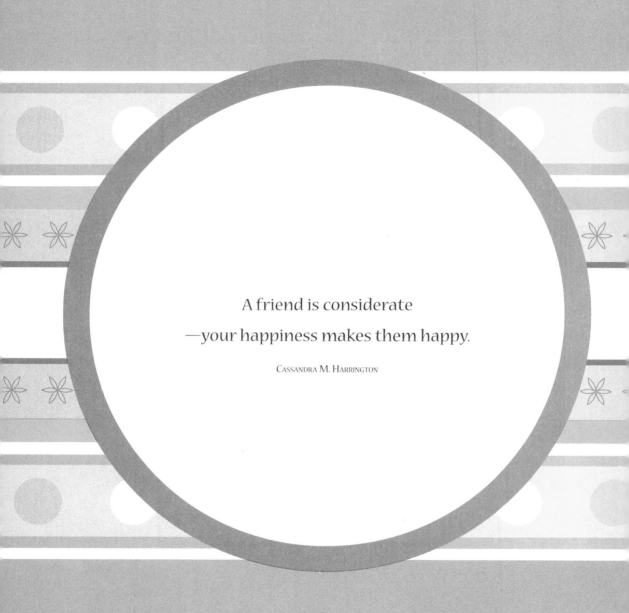

A friend is considerate

—your happiness makes them happy.

CASSANDRA M. HARRINGTON

THE ICING ON THE CAKE

By Carol McAdoo Rehme

Sharyn found life on the sidelines to be disconcerting.

Oh, sure, acquaintances stopped in, church members phoned regularly, and her sons kept in contact and ran errands. But she missed prowling the mall with girlfriends, participating in church meetings, even purchasing her own groceries. She missed running her own errands and puttering in the yard. She missed going. She missed doing.

And now, it seemed, she would miss her son's December wedding.

Sharyn had dealt with illness her entire life. As a newborn, she suffered from rickets, and her health only proceeded to worsen. Allergies, asthma, and other ailments hounded her until now, at fifty-five, her problems read like the index to a medical text: Arthritis. Bedsores. Collagen disease. Degenerative osteoporosis.

Sharyn needed heart and lung transplants but wasn't a candidate for either. Instead, committed to an elaborate schedule of pharmaceuticals, tethered to an oxygen tank, and confined to a wheelchair, Sharyn teased that she preferred spending her time traveling. Traveling between her two homes: the house and the hospital. Actually, going anywhere was out of the question, especially to her son's out-of-state wedding ceremony.

Because no plane, train, or car could accommodate Sharyn's delicate health needs, she resigned herself to staying home while the rest of the family attended the wedding . . . without her. They left her with tender promises to remember all the details, to take lots and lots of pictures, and to save her some wedding cake.

During her husband's absence, caregivers saw to her meals and personal needs, but Sharyn couldn't shake her blues and feelings of isolation. It wasn't easy finding herself apart from her family at Christmas and missing the festivities of her son's wedding. The hurt followed her as surely as the oxygen tube trailing her wheelchair.

But she hadn't counted on Vickie.

Vickie arrived with Big Plans: an old-fashioned girlfriends' slumber party. She surprised Sharyn by bringing along her own holiday guest, their mutual friend Carol. She supplied chocolates to nibble, popcorn to munch, sodas to drink . . . and a lively video to watch from bed later that night. The three gabbed and giggled away the hours, pausing only to click on the lamps when evening dimmed the room.

And they talked about everything under the sun—everything, that is, except the wedding Sharyn was missing.

Instead, the two women bundled their fragile friend against the bitter Kansas wind and, with meticulous timing and coordination, managed to pack Sharyn—wheelchair, oxygen tank, and all—into Vickie's van. Chirping like excited elves, the three headed out for their version of a night on the town: a tour of attractive Christmas displays scattered around the small-town neighborhoods. They *oohed* over animated vignettes. They *aahed* at each crèche.

They pointed out ribbon-wrapped wreaths, a window lit in peaceful blue, and a lawn festooned in red candy canes. But Vickie saved the best for last.

"Now, Sharyn, close your eyes while I turn the corner to this house." She maneuvered the car down the gravel road and stopped. "Okay, you can look."

Sharyn opened her eyes and gasped.

Sparkling, twinkling, and winking, thousands of tiny white lights outlined the winding drive like intricate frosting on a cake. A fantasy of winter white, they swagged the rows of arbors that canopied its entire length, like a powdering of a delicate angel dust.

The van inched its way under, through, and along the enchanting path; the women barely breathed, wide-eyed and wordless.

"Oh, look!" Sharyn whispered. "It's beautiful enough for a bride." Her voice caught. "Why, it's like a . . . a bridal arch!"

A sacred silence softened the air as all three pondered the thought.

"You know, Vickie," Sharyn murmured into the hush, "others will bring home a piece of the cake. But only a friend like *you* would bring me a piece of the wedding."[4]

Friendship is
a sheltering tree.

SAMUEL TAYLOR COLERIDGE

WHY I'M THANKFUL
YOU'RE MY BEST FRIEND...

...When you find a great T-shirt,

you buy me one too.

✴ ✴ ✴ ✴ ✴

Father,

You think of everything. From the beauty of the morning sunrise to colorful, fresh fruits and vegetables to strengthen my body to a warm place to sleep at night, You've given me everything I need to live a happy, fulfilling life. But one of the greatest blessings You've provided for me is the joy of friendship. You created us to need an intimate friendship with You as well as the companionship of others. And You've placed just the right friendships in my life to fill that need.

What's more, You give me opportunities to be a blessing to others by being a friend. Those moments when I can bring a smile to a friend's face or help my friends when they're in need are the greatest, most fulfilling times in my life. There is nothing more rewarding than to know I've brightened someone's day or relieved them of their burden in some small way.

Help me to take advantage of every opportunity You provide, both to have a friend and to be one. And most of all, thank You for considering me Your friend. May I never take our friendship for granted.

Amen.

I THANK GOD for you,

my THOUGHTFUL friend!

You're the

BEST
FRIEND
in the World Because...

We Share Each

Other's Dreams.

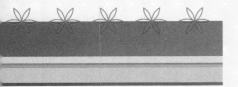

I'm treating you as a friend, asking you
to share my present minuses,
in the hope that I can ask you to share
my future pluses.

KATHERINE MANSFIELD

> *With God's power working in us, God can do much, much more than anything we can ask or imagine.*
>
> EPHESIANS 3:20 NCV

Do you have a friend who's always coming up with new ideas? If you haven't already, try jumping on board sometime and becoming a part of your friend's plans. Or maybe you need to share your own creative ideas with your friends. Creativity loves company, and we're able to accomplish so much more as a team.

God works through our friendships to bring us companionship, support, and sometimes to reveal more of Himself and His plan for us. Be open to the possibilities. Maybe you're good at forming ideas, and your friend is good at executing a plan. Together, you could accomplish much. Or maybe you enjoy doing crafts and preparing lessons for children, and your friend is good at public speaking. You could team up to lead a great Sunday school class.

Allow God to work through your friendships—He just may lead you and your friend into adventures you never would have embarked upon alone.

A LETTER TO MY FRIEND

Dear Friend,

I love the fact that we have so much fun sharing our thoughts and dreams with each other. Often when we get together, I may mention an idea I've been tossing around, wondering if it will work or even be possible, and before I know it, you have us in the middle of doing it. In your eyes, nothing is impossible. If it can be thought up, it can be done.

You've given me the courage to try new things that I never would have attempted on my own. You patiently put up with my occasional skepticism, using it as good exercise for your acute problem-solving skills. Many times we end up with a masterpiece and once in a while a flop, but we always learn much through the experience and have great fun and grow closer along the way.

Thank you for being my tenacious friend and for inspiring me to think outside the box. Your creative ideas and endless supply of optimism are such a blessing to me.

Love,

Your Friend

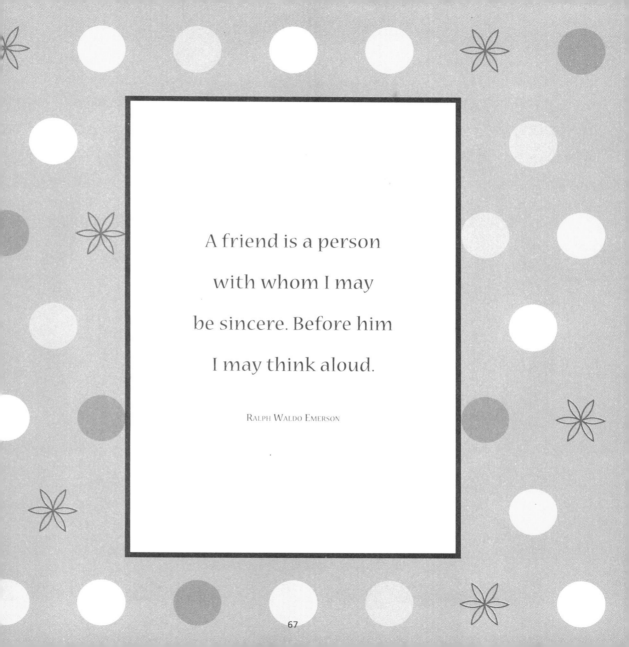

A friend is a person

with whom I may

be sincere. Before him

I may think aloud.

RALPH WALDO EMERSON

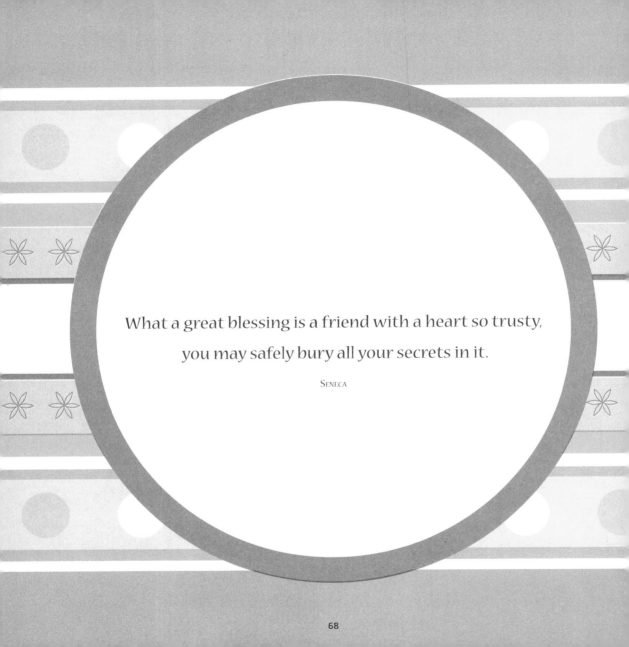

What a great blessing is a friend with a heart so trusty,
you may safely bury all your secrets in it.

SENECA

A PAIR OF SLIPPERS

BY BEV SCHELLENBERG

It started with a pair of slippers.

It was the first day of kindergarten. Excited, nervous, desperate for someone to be with once Mommy left me, I took the fuzzy blue slippers out of my bag. "May I put these next to yours?" I asked the tiny girl who stood beside me in the cloakroom, her hair as black as mine was blond. *It was okay to talk to this stranger,* I thought. Her mom and mine were in line, waiting to talk to the teacher, and they were talking.

"Yes, you can put your slippers here," she said, as she moved over her brown corduroy slippers along the ledge above the coatracks. Our slippers were inseparable after that, as were we. We fended off the class clown with our lunch buckets, narrowly missed being pounded by a class bully down at the tracks, ran together on the track team, played on opposite soccer teams at recess but had a secret pact to help each other, joked about her diminutive height, and performed as Snow White and the head dwarf in the school play. It was a united childhood, despite her strong Sikh upbringing and my just as strict Christian family background. She focused on sports while I found joy in practicing piano for three hours a day.

The day I told her I was adopted, she told her mom, "I want to be adopted, too." Twenty years later (after she'd grown taller than me), I met my birth mom, and she ran the poor woman through a battery of questions that would have made the FBI proud, all because my friend wanted to make sure this stranger wouldn't hurt me.

Little girls talking about the children they'd have, turned into teenagers worrying about the offspring they'd bring into the world. "What if I have a boy whose head is always stuck in a book, or a girl who only likes playing piano and singing?" she groaned.

"Well, what if I have a boy who only likes sports and a girl who hates reading?" I responded.

"We'll have to switch kids," we agreed.

We turned into professional women: her, a speech therapist; me, a music teacher and writer. Married with children, the connection remains. Rather than switch children, we exchange advice. At eight years old, her daughter is a natural musician, her head in the glorious clouds of imagination and idealism, while my daughter, same age, seems to always have her nose in a book. Her seven-year-old son is a natural basketball player, while my six-year-old son prefers golf and has a speech delay. Our individual training proved beneficial—by the time my beautiful son was two-and-a-half, she dared to tell me he had to have weekly speech therapy or end up severely speech disabled, and I dared to fill her in on her daughter's need for weekly music lessons and daily practice or she would end up miserable.

I still don't know a phoneme from phonics, and she doesn't know an eighth note from a middle C. But my son speaks fluently, and her daughter dances over the piano keys. And although the distance between our homes now spans the United States and Canada rather than a block, we remain united.

All because of a pair of slippers.[5]

Is there a dearer name than friend?
Think of it for me.

ABIGAIL ADAMS

＊ ＊ ＊ ＊ ＊

Lord,

It's great to have a friend who understands my dreams and who gets excited about them right along with me. When we get together, we love to talk about our latest ideas and dream about what we'll do in the future. Sometimes our dreams are big, like a new career we're considering; other times, they're small, maybe what color to paint the living room wall or a new system of organization one of us has come up with. Either way, it's fun to share a vision with someone and know that she's right there with me, seeing what I see.

You knew before we ever met each other that we had these similarities that would help us to understand each other so well. Thank You for bringing us across one another's paths and for creating such a meaningful friendship out of our common interests.

Bless my friend and all the dreams she has for her future, and thank You for allowing me to join her along her way.

Amen.

I THANK GOD for you,
my ENCOURAGING friend!

You're the

BEST
FRIEND
in the World Because...

You Believe the

Best in Me.

The proper office of a friend is to side with you when you are in the wrong. Nearly anybody will side with you when you are in the right.

MARK TWAIN

> *Love patiently accepts all things.*
> *It always trusts, always hopes, and*
> *always remains strong.*
>
> 1 Corinthians 13:7 ncv

Friends who love and accept us for who we are do wonders at boosting our confidence. Your friends weren't required to befriend you by any outside source; they chose you as the person they would like to share that special bond with because they see qualities in you that perhaps you don't always recognize in yourself.

Believe your friends when they compliment you and encourage you to use your God-given talents. Allow yourself to see who you are through their eyes. And make sure they know about the many great qualities you see in them as well.

Now that you've looked at yourself through your friends' eyes, try imagining what God sees when He looks at you. He sees a masterpiece—His own creation!

A LETTER TO MY FRIEND

Dear Friend,

You always seem to find the best in me, even in those things I consider faults. I've always thought of myself as a bit of a klutz, but you often comment on how you envy my gracefulness. What I see as being disorganized and messy, you see as a sort of creative genius in me.

When I'm around you, I feel witty because you seem to genuinely enjoy and laugh at my jokes. Your confidence in me pushes me to believe in myself and to try new things.

Thank you for being the kind of friend who sees the good in me and who finds even my faults endearing, loving me all the more for them. I hope you're able to see yourself the way I see you—as a beautiful, caring, fun-loving, outstanding woman and a genuine, supportive friend.

Love,

Your Friend

There's nothing as nice as a friend
who sees the good in you,
believes the best in you,
and encourages you to become the
beautiful person God made you to be!
You are that special friend to me.

CHARLOTTE MAE

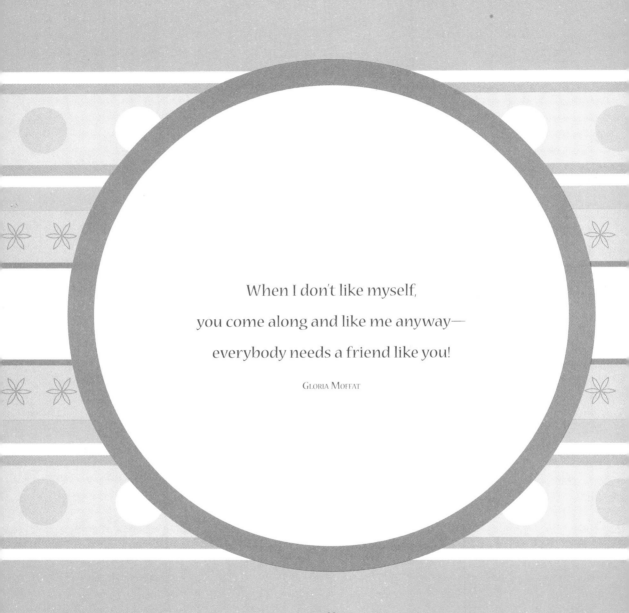

When I don't like myself,

you come along and like me anyway—

everybody needs a friend like you!

GLORIA MOFFAT

MY BUTTERFLY FRIEND

By Karen R. Kilby

Carol and Fred were newcomers to our church. I wanted her to feel welcome, so I invited her to attend the monthly ladies' luncheon with me. She hesitated. "I have a rare heart disease that can only be treated with experimental medication. I never know when I'm feeling up to doing something. I'd really like to, but I'd better not plan on it. I'm sorry."

I was disappointed. I had immediately liked her, and I wanted to get to know her better. She had such beautiful sparkling blue eyes and a smile that belied the fact that there was anything physically wrong with her.

As the months went by, we greeted each other in church, but every time an invitation was extended to do something, she refused. Still, Carol remained on my mind and in my heart, so I decided to try once more. This time, I invited her to attend a Bible study with me at another friend's home. "I don't even know if I could concentrate on the lesson. The heart medication slows everything down." Then, softly, she added, "I think I'd like to try."

As the weeks went by, Carol began to respond to the love shared at the study, and she participated more and more. Even when she wasn't feeling her best, she made the effort to attend, and we began to see a transformation. God was touching her heart, physically and spiritually.

One morning as we visited in the church foyer, my friend Darlene said, "Let's invite Carol to our pajama party!" This fun routine shared by Darlene and me had begun as a way to cure my loneliness when my husband was away on business trips. It seemed we never had enough time together, and there was always so much to talk and pray about. We invited Carol and were surprised and delighted when she said, "That sounds like fun! I'd love to come!"

She came through my door the next week with her arms loaded, then went back to the car to get her pajamas, pillow, comforter, teddy bear, and everything else she needed to feel at home away from home. The three of us talked until the wee hours of the morning and, after a late breakfast, continued to talk on into the afternoon, still in our pajamas.

Many more pajama parties followed. Each time, the guest room Carol occupied became more and more like home. Finally, she no longer needed to bring her pillow, comforter, and all the other things she clung to for solace. Like a butterfly, she was emerging out of her cocoon.

Miraculously, more adventures began. We started going on little outings, then bigger and bigger ones. The highlight of our escapades was the three of us taking an overnight trip to attend *Oprah.* Eventually, trips to Disney World on her own were second nature to her.

But when her daughter called announcing Carol's impending grand-motherhood, some of Carol's old doubts resurfaced: "Can I be the kind of grandma I want to be? I want to have fun with my babies. I want to babysit for them, rock them, hold them, and play with them." Carol's concerns about being physically able to care for her new grandson soon faded. The joy of holding him filled her heart to overflowing, and her caregiving took over. And with the second grandchild, her heart's capacity and her ability doubled.

Last week she called, exclaiming, "I'm going to Europe! Five days in Paris and five days in Austria to celebrate Holly and Andy's anniversary. They want me to come to watch the grandkids while they enjoy evenings out. My doctor has given me permission to go! Can you believe it?"

I do believe it. Girlfriends and pajama parties can really bring out the best in all of us.[6]

A real friend helps us
think our best thoughts,
do our noblest deeds,
be our finest selves.

AUTHOR UNKNOWN

WHY I'M THANKFUL YOU'RE MY BEST FRIEND...

...You think I'm smart, capable, clever, and pretty. You're my one-woman cheering section!

> *Best friend, my wellspring in the wilderness.*
>
> GEORGE ELIOT

✳ ✳ ✳ ✳ ✳

Heavenly Father,

When people spend a lot of time together, they tend to start getting annoyed by the little things—habits, personality quirks. Sometimes these little annoyances can turn into major conflicts.

Thank You for giving me friends who don't focus on the negative. They always see the best in me, many times pointing out positive characteristics or talents I didn't even know I had. Sure, we like to joke around with each other at times about the unique things that make us who we are, but it's always in a fun-loving way, never demeaning or hurtful. After all, our little quirks and differences are what make us special. My friends wouldn't be nearly as interesting to be around if they were all just like me.

Help me always to see the good in others and to take every opportunity to build up my friends. May each of them feel Your love today.

Amen.

I THANK GOD for you,

my BELIEVING friend!

You're the
BEST
FRIEND
in the World Because...

You Know
When to Talk and
When to Hug.

I was feeling bluer
than blue,
And then came you.
Understanding,
sympathy and a hug.
Then I was as good
as new.

OLIVIA SONG

How good is a timely word!

PROVERBS 15:23

Have you ever had someone offer just the right words of comfort when you needed it? It feels so good to know that someone truly understands. On the other hand, have you ever wished people would just be quiet because they really don't know what to say? In these cases, empty words of consolation can be more hurtful than helpful.

It's a rare gift to have the sensitivity to know when to speak and when to offer a quiet hug and a shoulder to cry on. This ability may come quite naturally to you. But if not, you can develop this ability with prayer and effort.

Pray for the wisdom to know what to say and the appropriate time to say it. If you don't know what to say, offer a hug, and be honest with your friend. She would probably much rather hear, "I don't know what to say, but I'm here for you for as long as you need me," than an empty platitude.

A TRIBUTE TO MY FRIEND

When my grandmother passed away after a lengthy battle with cancer, I was left with a void in my life. Not only did I miss her, but I also missed the hours I'd spent helping to care for her and the daily visits with her and her friends at the nursing home. I had plenty of supportive people around who offered me comfort, but the person who helped me through that time the most was a friend who said nothing, but offered a warm embrace.

In the coming weeks, she would call just to see how I was doing. Many times, we wouldn't even talk about my grandma, but her company lifted my spirits. She would find excuses to have me over to help her with little projects, filling my desire to be needed once again.

Thank You, Father, for sensitive friends who follow Your leading.

JORDAN FRANCIS

Women best

understand each

other's language.

SAINT TERESA OF AVILA

When words won't make a difference, a hug will.

Author Unknown

CANCER ANSWER

By Carol McAdoo Rehme

I collect experiences like others collect souvenirs. The only difference? I don't like to take them out, examine them, talk about them.

Oh, they're there just the same. Not stuck in the drawers of mind and memory. But out front, in plain view of the pitying eyes of uncomfortable family, friends, and strangers.

Cancer.

Even yet, the word is nearly unspeakable, like something foul, dirty, offensive. And, of course, scary. So scary, in fact, that I hesitate each time I say it aloud. Almost like it's one of the curse words my mother used to wash out of my mouth with soap. Or, even worse, I fear that saying it—outright saying it—makes it real.

Like it's not real? Silly me. Just look at the scars that grid my body. The swelling that distorts my face. The wisps of hair too sparse to cover my scalp.

I despise it.

The nausea, the fatigue, the sense of helplessness, the over-whelming hopelessness. The . . . loneliness. I feel so abandoned in my fight against this vicious intruder.

I did, that is, until I met Angelika.

Angelika never had cancer. She isn't a victim. She isn't a survivor. She's none of those titles usually tagged onto the "saviors" in stories like mine. Angelika is, quite simply, the most tenderhearted person I know. She's the new girl in town. Literally. And she moved in next door and right into the spot in my heart reserved for a best friend.

The first time we met, her eyes held no pity—they gleamed with interest. Interest in *me the person* as opposed to *me the cancer victim.* The "C" word wasn't something Angelika shied away from—any more than she shied away from *me.* Unlike others who chose to avoid me as if I were contagious.

Angelika filled—and continues to fill—my lonely spaces.

When I complain, she listens. When I hurt, she gives me bone-melting foot rubs. When I despair, she rents "hero" videos and encourages me to dissect them for their secrets. When I'm fatigued, she runs an errand or scrubs a toilet or sets out the garbage cans. When I'm cranky, she tells me "blonde" jokes and makes ridiculous faces and pokes fun at the world.

When I'm feeling well, she celebrates; when I cry, she cries with me.

Angelika.

Angel.

In my eyes, they are one and the same.[7]

Is there anything
more comforting than
talking with a friend over
a cup of tea?

Emma Chantelle

WHY I'M THANKFUL
YOU'RE MY BEST FRIEND...

...You make the world's

best cup of hot cocoa—

with plenty of marshmallows!

Friends are the sunshine of life.

JOHN HAY

⁕   ⁕   ⁕   ⁕   ⁕

Lord,

When I'm having a rough day, You always seem to know just which friend I need to talk to. On these days, I'll often get a phone call, and a caring voice will be on the other line. Sometimes my friend will help me laugh at the situation, and the tension will just melt away. Other times, she'll help me work out a solution. But many times, she'll just listen as I give vent to my emotions.

Thank You for friends who are sensitive to my needs and who don't just try to fill up silence with empty words. Sometimes, just a hug from a friend who really understands what I'm feeling is what I need the most. Thank You for working through the hands of my friends to remind me of Your constant love and care.

I surrender myself to You, Father. Please work through me to express Your great love to my dear friends.

Amen.

I THANK GOD for you,

    my UNDERSTANDING friend!

You're the

BEST

FRIEND

in the World Because...

You Share Your
Heart.

I suppose there is
one friend in the life
of each of us
who seems not a
separate person,
however dear and beloved,
but an expansion,
an interpretation,
of one's self,
the very meaning
of one's soul.

EDITH WHARTON

* *

Dear friends, let us love one another,
for love comes from God. Everyone who loves
has been born of God and knows God.

1 JOHN 4:7

Loving and being loved by others requires a certain amount of openness, a willingness to be honest with others and with ourselves about who we really are. It's difficult to feel close to a friend who keeps you at a distance, never revealing deep thoughts or feelings. But those who are honest about themselves usually find it easy to make friends and relate with others.

If you have trouble opening up to people, perhaps the best place to start is in getting to better know the way God sees you. The Bible offers many insights into God's view of you. You are completely loved and accepted by Him, and there is nothing you can do to change His mind about you. And God doesn't expect you to be perfect either. As you learn to see yourself in the light of God's grace, it's easy to let others see and know you as well.

* *

A LETTER TO MY FRIEND

Dear Friend,

You are that one person from whom I can never hide anything, and you're just as transparent with me. When one of us is hurting, all it takes is a simple "How are you?" on the phone for the tears to start flowing and the healing power of sharing one's heart with another to begin. When I'm excited about something, you're the first person I want to call, and you're always glad to share in my joy. If I need advice, I know you'll be completely honest with me; you won't just tell me what I want to hear. I know I can tell you anything, and it won't change your opinion of me at all, and I'm sure you know you can be as open with me without any fear of being judged.

I'm so grateful to have you as my friend and for the close connection we share.

Love,

Your Friend

In my friend

I find a second self.

ISABEL NORTON

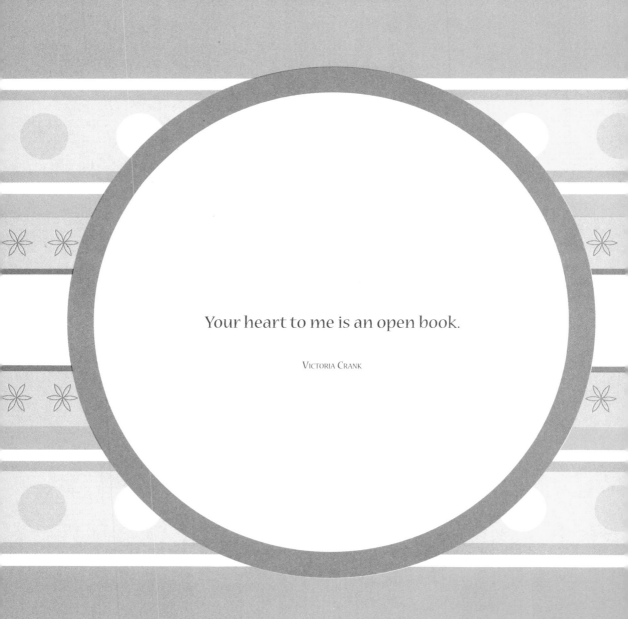

Your heart to me is an open book.

Victoria Crank

JOYCIE

By Sally Friedman

My best friend's voice never changes. Even if Joycie's hair has turned to silver and there are "character lines" where once there were none, my oldest childhood friend has the same low-key, reassuring voice that she's always had.

I heard it again on her birthday because come what may, we always manage to find one another when it matters.

Joycie and I live in distant cities, which makes our connection difficult geographically. And talk about opposites . . . from all outward appearances, there is no reason why this friendship should survive. Not with our diametrically opposite natures, habits, lifestyles, and ideas.

But when you have shared childhood with someone—when that someone lived in the next house from yours and knows your past, your parents, and your secrets—well, then, logic is not the issue.

Joycie was the first person I wanted to tell about the man I would ultimately marry.

It was Joycie I needed to talk to when my father died, and Joycie who understood all of my agony and ecstasy at becoming a mother. In that department, I beat her by years . . . yet we ended up having grandchildren on the very same day, which we regard as part of a cosmic master plan. I like to think that many women and some lucky men have the same precious thing we share: a bond that is marrow-deep, that will survive time and distance and circumstance and nearly any obstacle you can name because it is rooted in a profound connection.

I love Joycie. I worry about her health and the state of her second marriage, so much more stable than her first, but still plagued with unexpected problems. I worry about the welfare of her beautiful daughter and her wonderful son.

I exult in Joycie's successes.

I ache for her sorrows.

I tease her mercilessly about her compulsive cleaning, an area in which we surely part company.

But under the teasing is affection, understanding, and a loyalty that is so unquestioned and unquestionable that I know Joycie would be by my side instantly if I needed her, just as I would fly to hers.

"So, are you well?" I ask Joycie on this midlife birthday. And as I exhale, she says that yes, she is . . . despite anxiety about ten pounds that won't go away and upper arms that flap in the breeze.

We compare notes, go through the minor league stuff, then spend a few minutes exploring the rest—the overwhelming, scary imponderables.

Joycie knows all the chinks in my armor; I know all of hers. And we both understand that while we used to think we'd be past the deforming fears we shared as kids, grown-ups get scared, too.

Somewhere toward the end of our birthday chat, one of us will sigh and remember life before all this.

We'll drift back to Arlington Street and our childhood houses, sifting through the memories that grow more cherished with each birthday.

We'll swear that soon, soon, we'll take that trip to Paris that we used to dream about when she was twelve and I was ten and we watched too many movies together.

I'll wish my best friend the best year ever. I'll get a little misty as I tell her so.

And then we'll return to our lives, nourished by the sweet and wonderful nectar of a friendship that just keeps getting better—and the knowledge that if we have to be getting older, it's nice to do it together.[8]

Forget injuries; never forget kindnesses.

CONFUCIUS

❋ ❋ ❋ ❋ ❋

Heavenly Father,

I treasure the honesty and openness in the friendships You've placed in my life. I never feel that I need to put on an act or be anyone other than myself when I'm around my friends. It's a great feeling to be loved and accepted for who I am, not for a false image someone has of me or what I can do for that person.

Thank You for being that kind of friend. Sometimes I'm tempted to try to put on airs when I talk to You, as if I need to be someone other than myself—someone better—to enter into Your presence. But our best times together are when I'm completely honest with You, bringing just who I am before You, faults and all. And every time, You assure me of Your unconditional love toward me.

It's a great feeling to know and be known by my friends and an even greater joy to know and be known by You, my Creator, loving Father, and constant Friend.

Amen.

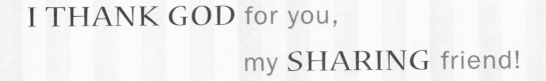

I THANK GOD for you,
my SHARING friend!

You're the

BEST

FRIEND

in the World Because...

You Challenge Me
to Be My Best.

Your acceptance helps me
accept myself—but your example
spurs me on to greater heights.

R. Norton

❋ ❋ ❋ ❋ ❋ ❋ ❋ ❋ ❋ ❋ ❋ ❋ ❋ ❋ ❋ ❋ ❋

The pleasantness of one's friend springs from his earnest counsel.

PROVERBS 27:9

Friends have a way of making those things we really need to hear a bit more palatable. For some reason, a word of advice is often easier to accept from a friend than from a parent, sibling, or even sometimes a pastor or mentor. A close friend invests in your heart and, as a result, is concerned not only with your physical and spiritual well-being but with your emotional happiness as well. And because your friends' backgrounds often differ from your own, they bring a unique perspective and may recognize things you might never see in yourself. They may push you out of your comfort zone, which could be exactly where God is wanting you to go.

A friend whom you can confide in and turn to for sound advice is a precious treasure. No friend will have all the answers, but they can certainly be the tool God uses to lead you to the answers He has for you.

❋ ❋ ❋ ❋ ❋ ❋ ❋ ❋ ❋ ❋ ❋ ❋ ❋ ❋ ❋ ❋ ❋

A LETTER TO MY FRIEND

Dear Friend,

You never let me settle for mediocre. In your gentle, caring way, you push me toward a greater goal than I would dare to set for myself. When I become weary of my busy schedule, you help me see how to take some time out for fun, weed out activities that are unimportant, and manage my important obligations bit by bit so I don't feel so overwhelmed. When my children try my nerves, you remind me of how much I would miss were I not so involved in their lives. My time with them goes all too quickly, and you teach me by your example how to savor every moment.

Thank you for challenging me to be my best and for allowing God to work through you to mold me into the person He wants me to be.

Love,

Your Friend

The greatest good

you can do for another

is not just share

your riches, but to reveal

to him his own.

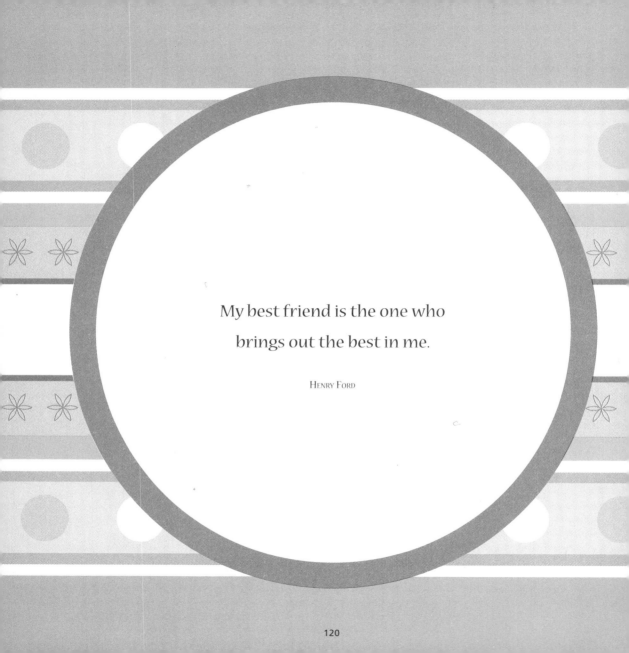

My best friend is the one who
brings out the best in me.

HENRY FORD

BURGER KING

By Teena Myers

I stomped out of the church. Threw the clipboard on the backseat of my car and slammed the door. Enough was enough. I fumbled in my purse for Advil and swallowed two, before speeding out of the parking lot.

"How dare they fire me!" I grumbled. "They didn't hire me. I volunteered. You can't fire a volunteer!"

I pulled into my driveway and fished for my cell phone, flipped it open, and dialed my best friend's number.

"Hello, Kathy. You won't believe what just happened."

"What?" Kathy's voice filled with concern. I immediately felt better. Kathy had a way of knowing what I needed.

"The play is ruined. I told them a black backdrop would offset the white angel costumes. Do you know what color it is?"

"No," said Kathy.

"Blue! The yellow crowns I donated are being painted silver, and they think the angels should wear sandals." I paused, so Kathy could agree. Silence. I continued. "Three shows, I told them, three, but no, they only want to do one show. Kathy, are you there?"

"Yes, Teena. I'm listening."

"They assigned Mary and Joseph's parts to children. Adults should play those parts." I paused for her agreement. More silence. "Kathy."

"Teena," Kathy said. "You are just like Burger King."

"What does that mean?"

"You want it your way."

Stunned by her response, I hung up without saying good-bye and stared at the phone. Kathy was the kindest, most sensitive person I knew. I couldn't imagine what had possessed her to say something so hurtful. I wiped the tears from my face and went inside.

I tossed my purse on the desk. The picture of Dan and me at the beach glared at me. I slid the cell phone into my pocket, picked up the picture, and wiped away some dust. Dan had wanted to go to Alaska, but I insisted on Hawaii. He looked sad in this picture. I put the picture in the desk drawer and headed for the bedroom.

On the way to the bedroom, I tripped over the ottoman. The brown leather ottoman that matched the leather furniture and was the reason for the worst fight I ever had with Dan. He wanted deep-cushioned blue furniture. I insisted on leather. It was easier to clean, and I did the housework. I never understood why he had been so stubborn and unreasonable.

Uneasiness stirred within me. I ran to the bedroom and slammed the door. My heart raced, and I backed against the door to hold it shut as though some evil creature were chasing me. "I'm safe in here," I whispered. The green bedspread covered with delicate pink flowers glowed, and I shielded my eyes. Dan had wanted stripes.

I slowly slid down the door until seated on the floor and burst into tears. The sickening truth screamed at me from every corner of the room. I wanted the oak bed. I wanted the wicker chairs. I wanted the cream carpet. Kathy was right. I pulled the phone out of my pocket and quickly dialed her number. "Kathy, you are the best friend I've ever had."[9]

Don't make friends who are comfortable to be with.
Make friends who will force you to become better
than who you are today.

THOMAS J. WATSON SR.

✲　✲　✲　✲　✲

Lord,

My friends are great encouragers. They're always there to applaud my successes and to bolster my confidence when I'm feeling down. But something I appreciate most about them is their willingness to be completely honest with me and to give me a little push in the right direction when I need it. If I'm having a pity party, they sympathize with me but don't join in on the party. Instead, they often remind me of all the ways I've been blessed. If I'm getting too wrapped up in my own to-do list to make time for what You want to do in my life, they're good to give me a kind little reminder and help me get back to what really matters.

Another thing I admire about my friends is that they are continually striving to be their very best at whatever they do, and they truly desire to please You. Just being around them makes me feel motivated and energized.

Thank You for giving me such dedicated and honest friends. Pour Your blessings into their lives as they follow You, and help me to be an encourager and motivator for each of them as well.

Amen.

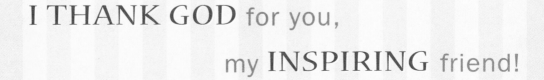

I THANK GOD for you,

my INSPIRING friend!

JOURNAL FOR TWO

A good friend and a journal serve similar functions in your life: you tell them both secrets you'd never share with anyone else. Why not share one with the other? Make a joint investment in a blank book—lined if you're linear; unlined if you're free-form types. Then take turns making entries, passing the book back and forth. If you're lucky enough to be living in close proximity, you can trade off every time you see each other. If your friendship is geographically challenged, use the exchange to shrink the distance between you and to keep you feeling close and connected.

BEST FRIENDS

By Sally Clark

I don't know what I was looking for
when I walked into your shop that day,
a card, I think, and certainly not a
friend, but there you were when
your phone rang, your daughter calling
to cry her disappointment in a "B" on one of
her papers and I laughed and said a "B"
would be a blessing from my son
in the same grade.

Breakfast being the only time we
could share a meal, you had to cancel
the first time, but I insisted on another day,
and you never know, when things get started,
how nourishing they might become,
meeting once a week, consuming so much
more than coffee.
Never coffee.
Dr. Pepper and hot tea more to taste,
bacon and no eggs,
lots of cheese and fruit, please, but
there was a phase

with hamburgers
that we won't mention now.
We set the table every week with
the hungers in our hearts;
spreading out children, jobs, and faith;
chewing over husbands lost and loved;
blessing one another with our listening;
sprinkling salty tears into paper napkins we left
behind for others to throw away;
laughter sweetening every bite.

How many blessings are left
for us to savor after all these many years,
we cannot know;
but my prayer is that we'll break bread and
chew the fat and celebrate for
many years to come,
our morning worship;
blessing and being blessed;
you taught me to
say grace.[10]

NOTES

[1] Julie Morrison, Sunbury, Ohio. Story used by permission of author.
[2] Carol McAdoo Rehme, Loveland, Colorado. Story used by permission of author.
[3] Sue Dunigan, St. Croix, U.S. Virgin Islands. Story used by permission of author.
[4] Carol McAdoo Rehme, Loveland, Colorado. Story used by permission of author.
[5] Bev Schellenberg, Surrey, BC, Canada. Story used by permission of author.
[6] Karen R. Kilby, Kingwood, Texas. Story used by permission of author.
[7] Carol McAdoo Rehme, Loveland, Colorado. Story used by permission of author.
[8] Sally Friedman, Moorestown, New Jersey. Story used by permission of author.
[9] Teena Myers, Westwego, Louisiana. Story used by permission of author.
[10] Sally Clark, Fredericksburg, Texas. Poem used by permission of author.

LOOK FOR THESE BOOKS:

THE BEST GRANDMA
IN THE WORLD

THE BEST SISTER
IN THE WORLD

THE BEST TEACHER
IN THE WORLD

HOWARD BOOKS
A DIVISION OF SIMON & SCHUSTER
New York   London   Toronto   Sydney